TEN KEYS FOR UNLOCKING THE BIBLE COURSE
PARTICIPANT GUIDE

Colin S. Smith

MOODY PUBLISHERS
Chicago

© 2003 by COLIN S. SMITH

Interior design by Kelly Wilson, Paetzold Associates, Inc.,
St. Charles, Illinois.

ISBN: 0-8024-6549-8
ISBN-13: 978-0-8024-6549-8

We hope you enjoy this book from Moody Publishers.
Our goal is to provide high-quality, thought-provoking
books and products that connect truth to your real needs
and challenges. For more information on other books
and products written and produced from a biblical
perspective, go to www.moodypublishers.com or write to:

Moody Publishers
820 N. LaSalle Boulevard
Chicago, IL 60610

5 7 9 10 8 6 4

Printed in the United States of America

Study Guide

INTRODUCTION

Welcome to the *Ten Keys for Unlocking the Bible Course*.

If you want to connect with God and are interested in what the Bible has to say, but you don't know where to begin, the *Ten Keys* study is for you.

The Bible is the world's best-selling book, but it is long and sometimes difficult to understand. The *Ten Keys for Unlocking the Bible* video series will give you a place to begin. This video program is rather like a high-altitude flight over a range of mountains. You will see what the ground looks like and get a good glimpse of the highest peaks.

The ten keys highlighted in this video series will help you to understand who you are and what gives your life meaning and significance. They will help you to make sense of this world with its great joys and shattering disappointments. They will help you to know God and show you how He has been reaching out to men and women throughout the Bible story, and how He is still reaching out to you today. Finally, these ten keys will introduce you to Jesus Christ, showing how His life, death, and resurrection can give you hope, purpose, and power for today.

I am grateful to my colleague Greg Norwine for his partnership in developing this study guide. Our hope and prayer is that in discovering the world of the Bible, you will encounter the Living God.

Now get ready for a fascinating and life-changing journey.

How to Use This Study Guide

This study guide is designed for use with the *Ten Keys for Unlocking the Bible* video series.

Each study begins by "Setting the Scene." This will show you where you are in the Bible story and give you some helpful background information. You may want to read this section before viewing the video, or you may choose to skip it altogether.

"Following Along" provides an outline for each presentation that will help you to remember what you have learned. You may like to add your own notes on these pages.

"Discussing Together" will help your group to interact with the main points of the presentation and apply the Bible's teaching to your own life. Discussion is an important and enjoyable aspect of the *Ten Keys* study. You should feel free to share your questions and insights during this time. Everyone in the group has something to offer. But don't feel under any pressure. Some people are more comfortable sitting back and taking it all in.

"Building the Story" gives a one-sentence summary of the topic you have just covered. These summaries will help you to see how the Bible fits together. You will find it helpful to review these points from time to time as you progress through the study. A complete list of the "Building the Story" points can be found on pages 107–108.

The *Ten Keys* study does not require any advance preparation, but the "Looking Ahead" section previews what is coming; so if you would like, you may read the relevant chapter from the Bible before your next session.

Key Number One

THE GARDEN

SETTING THE SCENE

*O*UR aim in these ten studies is to explain what the Bible teaches. Of course, we would like you to believe the Bible, but before you can make that decision, you need to know what it says.

Coming to a *Ten Keys* study is like being invited into a house and shown around its rooms. We want you to experience the world of the Bible and to see how it all connects together.

You won't be told what to believe, but you will discover what the Bible teaches, and you will learn about the living God who introduces Himself through the Scriptures.

We begin our study in Genesis, the first book of the Bible. Genesis literally means "beginnings." And in the book of Genesis we discover the beginnings of the universe, animals, the human race, marriage, the family, nations, governments, music, agriculture, cities, and languages.

We don't know exactly *when* these events took place, but the Bible does give us a hint as to *where* they occurred. The Garden of Eden was near the Tigris and Euphrates Rivers (Genesis 2:14). These rivers may have altered their course, but assuming that they are the same as those in the days of Adam and Eve, the original Garden of Eden was somewhere in the vicinity of modern-day Iraq.

The events that took place in the Garden of Eden are our first key for unlocking the Bible.

POSSIBLE LOCATION OF THE GARDEN OF EDEN

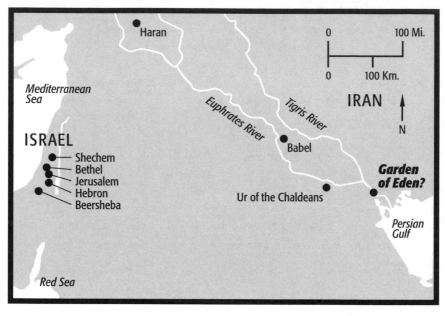

Dates	Events	Books of the Bible	World History
	Creation	Genesis	
	The Flood		
			Construction of pyramids begins in Egypt (2650 B.C.)
		Job	
2000 B.C.	Abraham	Genesis	Metalworkers create bronze, ushering in Bronze Age
	Isaac		
	Jacob		
	Four Hundred Years of Slavery in Egypt	Exodus	
1500 B.C.	Exodus from Egypt (Moses)	Exodus, Leviticus, Numbers, Deuteronomy	Egyptians begin using parchment for writing
	Entrance into Canaan (Joshua)	Joshua	
	Three Hundred Years of Chaos (the Judges)	Judges Ruth	King Tut buried with fabulous treasures in Egypt
1000 B.C.	King Saul King David King Solomon	1 and 2 Samuel, 1 and 2 Kings, 1 Chronicles (Psalms, Proverbs, Ecclesiastes, Song of Songs)	
	Divided Kingdom (930 B.C.)	Isaiah, Jeremiah, Lamentations, Ezekiel, Daniel and the Minor Prophets	First Olympic Games held at Olympia in Greece
500 B.C.	Fall of Jerusalem and exile		Aesop becomes famous for his fables
	Rebuilding of Jerusalem (Ezra, Nehemiah)	Ezra, Nehemiah, Esther	Plato born in Greece
			Great Wall of China completed
4 B.C.	Birth of Christ		

FOLLOWING ALONG

INTRODUCTION:
The whole Bible is one story that points to Jesus Christ.

I. God Is the Creator.

In the beginning God created the heavens and the earth. (Genesis 1:1)

A. The Creator is the owner.

B. Being created gives your life meaning and purpose.

C. Being created in God's image gives you unique value.

Then God said, "Let us make man in our image." (Genesis 1:26)

II. God Gives Good Gifts.

A. God gives His presence.

Then the man and his wife heard the sound of the LORD God as he was walking in the garden in the cool of the day. (Genesis 3:8)

B. God gives a place. (See the map on page 10.)

Now the LORD God had planted a garden in the east, in Eden; and there he put the man he had formed. (Genesis 2:8)

C. God gives a purpose.

Now the LORD God had formed out of the ground all the beasts of the field and all the birds of the air. He brought them to the man to see what he would name them; and whatever the man called each living creature, that was its name. (Genesis 2:19)

D. God gives a partner.

> *The LORD God said, "It is not good for the man to be alone. I will make a helper suitable for him." . . . The LORD God made a woman from the rib he had taken out of the man, and he brought her to the man. (Genesis 2:18, 22)*

III. Human Beings Have Become Alienated from God.

A. God gave one command.

> *"You must not eat from the tree of the knowledge of good and evil." (Genesis 2:17)*

B. The first man and woman chose the knowledge of evil, and evil became a power in human nature.

C. The two were excluded from God's presence.

> *So the LORD God banished him from the Garden of Eden. (Genesis 3:23)*

IV. God Has Made the Way Back.

A. God consigned the enemy to destruction.

> *God said to the serpent, ". . . Cursed are you." (Genesis 3:14)*

B. In God's mercy, Adam's curse was deflected.

> *"Cursed is the ground because of you." (Genesis 3:17)*

C. Jesus came to become a curse for us.

> *Christ redeemed us . . . by becoming a curse for us. (Galatians 3:13)*

DISCUSSING TOGETHER

1. What have you inherited from your parents for which you are thankful?

2. What difference does it make whether you were created by God or are an accident of history? What are the implications of each?

3. How do you explain the great pain, suffering, and strife that we see in our world today?

_____

_____

_____

_____

_____

4. How have you seen God's hand in providing a place, a purpose, or a partner for you?

_____

_____

_____

_____

_____

5. Would you like a greater sense of God's presence in your life? Why or why not?

_____

_____

_____

_____

_____

_____

_____

Building the Story

THE GARDEN:
God created Adam and Eve in His image, but they chose to disobey Him, gained the knowledge of evil, and were evicted from Paradise.

Looking Ahead

If you would like to prepare in advance for session two, read the Ten Commandments found in Exodus 20. As you read, consider why God might have given these particular commandments to His people.

Key Number Two

THE LAW

SETTING THE SCENE

*T*WO things happened after Adam and Eve were driven from the Garden.

The first was that evil got worse. It had taken root in human nature and brought great suffering, pain, and death to the human race. Eventually, God brought a worldwide flood to cut back the progress of evil that otherwise threatened to destroy the whole of humanity.

The second was that God kept reaching out to men and women. God had promised that a deliverer would come to save us from the knowledge of evil and restore God's presence and blessing. The Bible story shows us how God is faithful to His promise.

God made Himself known to a man by the name of Abraham, promising to bless him and bring blessing to the whole world through him (Genesis 12:2–3). From this point onward, the Bible story focuses on the descendants of Abraham.

During a great famine, Abraham's grandson Jacob and his entire family settled in Egypt, where there was grain. Their descendants remained there and eventually became enslaved and oppressed. Over a period of four hundred years, Jacob's descendants grew in number from the seventy original family members to a people numbering nearly two million.

God had compassion on these people and acted to deliver them. He raised up Moses, who led them out of Egypt and back to the land God had promised to Abraham. Along the way, these two million Hebrew people stopped at Mount Sinai, where God made a covenant with them, in which He said, " I will walk among you and be your God, and you will be my people" (Leviticus 26:12). Then God gave them the Ten Commandments.

THE ROUTE OF THE EXODUS TO MOUNT SINAI

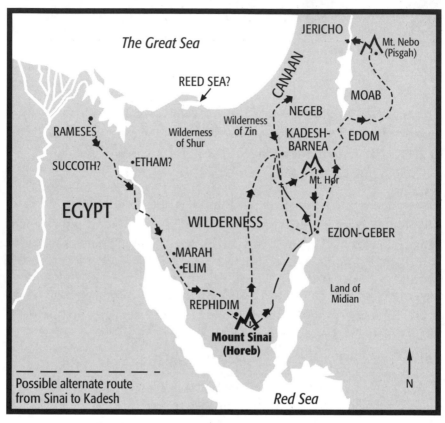

Moses led the Hebrew people out of Egypt to Mount Sinai, where God gave them the Ten Commandments.

DATES	EVENTS	BOOKS OF THE BIBLE	WORLD HISTORY
	Creation	Genesis	
	The Flood		
			Construction of pyramids begins in Egypt (2650 B.C.)
		Job	
2000 B.C.	Abraham	Genesis	Metalworkers create bronze, ushering in Bronze Age
	Isaac		
	Jacob		
	Four Hundred Years of Slavery in Egypt	Exodus	
	Exodus from Egypt (Moses)	Exodus, Leviticus, Numbers, Deuteronomy	Egyptians begin using parchment for writing
	Entrance into Canaan (Joshua)	Joshua	
	Three Hundred Years of Chaos (the Judges)	Judges Ruth	King Tut buried with fabulous treasures in Egypt
1000 B.C.	King Saul King David King Solomon	1 and 2 Samuel, 1 and 2 Kings, 1 Chronicles (Psalms, Proverbs, Ecclesiastes, Song of Songs)	
	Divided Kingdom (930 B.C.)	Isaiah, Jeremiah, Lamentations, Ezekiel, Daniel and the Minor Prophets	First Olympic Games held at Olympia in Greece
500 B.C.	Fall of Jerusalem and exile		Aesop becomes famous for his fables
	Rebuilding of Jerusalem (Ezra, Nehemiah)	Ezra, Nehemiah, Esther	Plato born in Greece
			Great Wall of China completed
4 B.C.	Birth of Christ		

FOLLOWING ALONG

I. God Gave the Ten Commandments.

1. "You shall have no other gods before me" (Exodus 20:3).

2. "You shall not make for yourself an idol" (v. 4).

3. "You shall not misuse the name of the LORD your God" (v. 7).

4. "Remember the Sabbath day by keeping it holy" (v. 8).

5. "Honor your father and your mother" (v. 12).

6. "You shall not murder" (v. 13).

7. "You shall not commit adultery" (v. 14).

8. "You shall not steal" (v. 15).

9. "You shall not give false testimony" (v. 16).

10. "You shall not covet" (v. 17).

II. There Is Purpose in God's Law.

A. God's Law is like a mirror reflecting the character of God.

1. Since they were His people, their lives must be modeled on who He is.

2. Without God, there is no foundation for the commandments.

3. Many people want to be good without God, but God defines what is good.

4. When you see how the law reflects God's character, your reaction will be to worship Him.

B. God's Law is like an X ray reflecting our primary struggles.

   1. The commandments speak to the ten most significant struggles of human life.

   2. The first four commandments reflect our struggle to love God.

   3. The last six commandments reflect our struggle to love our neighbor as ourselves.

   4. The Law, like an X ray, reveals problems of which we are not aware.

C. God's Law is like a railway track giving direction for your life.

   1. God wants your life to reflect His character.

   2. The Holy Spirit can create a desire to follow God's laws within you.

     I will give you a new heart and put a new spirit in you. . . . And I will put my Spirit in you and move you to follow my decrees and be careful to keep my laws. (Ezekiel 36:26–27)

   3. The Holy Spirit can give you power to move in the direction of God's commands.

   4. The Holy Spirit turns God's commands into promises.

DISCUSSING TOGETHER

1. What was one of the big rules of your household, growing up?

_____

_____

2. In what ways did this lesson change your perspective of the Ten Commandments?

_____

_____

_____

_____

_____

_____

3. If God dropped the Ten Commandments into an isolated people group that knew nothing about Him, how do you think it would impact their lives?

_____

_____

_____

_____

_____

_____

_____

4. Which of the Ten Commandments do you think are most difficult for people to obey? Why?

_____

_____

_____

_____

_____

_____

5. In what sense is the Law an X ray of our soul? What do you think it will reveal about the condition of our souls?

_____

_____

_____

_____

_____

6. If the X ray of the Law shows our souls to be seriously sick, what hope is there for us?

_____

_____

_____

_____

_____

_____

Building the Story

THE LAW:
The Ten Commandments reflect the character of God, identify our greatest struggles, and demonstrate our need for Jesus Christ.

Looking Ahead

If you would like to prepare in advance for session three, read Leviticus 16. It describes the Day of Atonement, a religious ceremony instituted by God to illustrate how He would deal with our sins. Imagine how you would have felt if you were observing this ceremony.

Key Number Three

THE SACRIFICE

SETTING THE SCENE

*W*HEN God gave the Ten Commandments, He also gave the sacrificial system to His people. The commandments set out how God's people were to live. The sacrifices illustrated how God's people would be forgiven.

God gave Moses precise details for building the tabernacle. It was a mobile worship center divided into different areas by a series of curtains. At the center of the tabernacle was an area called "the Most Holy Place."

If you had gone into the Most Holy Place (though nobody but the high priest ever did), you would have seen the ark of the covenant. It was a wooden chest carried on poles and covered by a lid. The stones on which God had written the Ten Commandments were kept inside.

On top of the ark were two golden statues depicting cherubim—the angelic figures who had guarded the entrance to the Garden of Eden. Between these rising figures was an area called the "atonement cover," or the "mercy seat."

Only one person, the high priest, was allowed to go into the Most Holy Place, and he did so only on the Day of Atonement.

What happened on that day was a powerful visual presentation of the Bible's central message.

THE ARK OF THE COVENANT

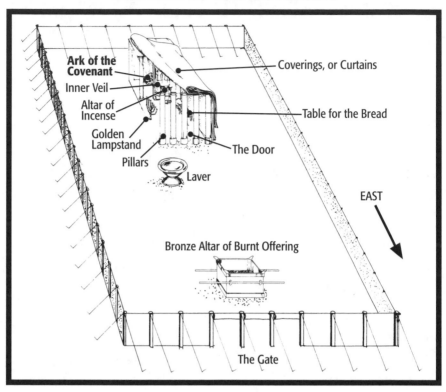

The ark of the covenant housed in the Most Holy Place was the centerpiece of Israelite worship. This was where God promised to meet with the high priest on the Day of Atonement.

DATES	EVENTS	BOOKS OF THE BIBLE	WORLD HISTORY
	Creation	Genesis	
	The Flood		
			Construction of pyramids begins in Egypt (2650 B.C.)
		Job	
2000 B.C.	Abraham	Genesis	Metalworkers create bronze, ushering in Bronze Age
	Isaac		
	Jacob		
	Four Hundred Years of Slavery in Egypt	Exodus	
1500 B.C.	Exodus from Egypt (Moses)	Exodus, Leviticus, Numbers, Deuteronomy	Egyptians begin using parchment for writing
	Entrance into Canaan (Joshua)	Joshua	
	Three Hundred Years of Chaos (the Judges)	Judges Ruth	King Tut buried with fabulous treasures in Egypt
1000 B.C.	King Saul King David King Solomon	1 and 2 Samuel, 1 and 2 Kings, 1 Chronicles (Psalms, Proverbs, Ecclesiastes, Song of Songs)	
	Divided Kingdom (930 B.C.)	Isaiah, Jeremiah, Lamentations, Ezekiel, Daniel and the Minor Prophets	First Olympic Games held at Olympia in Greece
500 B.C.	Fall of Jerusalem and exile		Aesop becomes famous for his fables
	Rebuilding of Jerusalem (Ezra, Nehemiah)	Ezra, Nehemiah, Esther	Plato born in Greece
			Great Wall of China completed
4 B.C.	Birth of Christ		

FOLLOWING ALONG

INTRODUCTION:

    A. The people broke the Ten Commandments while God was giving them to Moses.

    B. When we break God's Law, it leads to alienation from Him.

    C. How can God's presence be restored?

        1. Being sorry will not bring back God's presence and blessing.

        2. God's answer was illustrated in the drama of the Day of Atonement.

I. The High Priest Illustrates Atonement in Action (Leviticus 16).
Act 1: The priest appears.

    In place of his magnificent uniform, he was dressed as a common slave.

Act 2: The priest prepares.

    He offered a bull as a sacrifice for his own sins.

Act 3: Atonement is made.

    a. Atonement is "what needs to be done to put what is wrong right."

    b. The high priest took the blood of a sacrificed animal into the Most Holy Place.

    He shall then slaughter the goat for the sin offering for the people and take its blood behind the curtain and . . . sprinkle it on the atonement cover. (Leviticus 16:15)

Act 4: Sin is confessed.

He is to lay both hands on the head of the live goat and confess over it all the wickedness and rebellion of the Israelites—all their sins—and put them on the goat's head. (Leviticus 16:21)

Act 5: Guilt is removed.

He shall send the goat away into the desert in the care of a man appointed for the task. The goat will carry on itself all their sins to a solitary place. (Leviticus 16:21–22)

II. Jesus Makes Atonement.

Act 1: Christ appeared.

He was wrapped in strips of cloth and laid in a manger.

Act 2: Christ prepared.

He lived a perfect life without sin.

Act 3: Christ made atonement.

His blood was shed at the cross.

Act 4: Confession is made.

When we lay hold of Christ by faith, He takes our sins away.

Act 5: Guilt is removed.

When Christ takes our sins, our guilt is removed.

*For as high as the heavens are above the earth,
so great is his love for those who fear him;
as far as the east is from the west,
so far has he removed our transgressions from us.
(Psalm 103:11–12)*

DISCUSSING TOGETHER

1. How do you think most people deal with their feelings of guilt?

2. If you had been in the crowd watching on the Day of Atonement, what would have impressed you most?

3. Why could God not have just forgiven the people without going through this elaborate ceremony? What does this tell you about His character?

4. The high priest confessed the sins of the people in his prayer. Is it important for us to confess our sins today? And if so, how should we do that?

_____

_____

_____

_____

_____

_____

_____

5. What new insights did you gain from this message about Jesus' life and death?

_____

_____

_____

_____

_____

_____

_____

_____

_____

_____

_____

_____

_____

Building the Story

THE SACRIFICE:

Through the Day of Atonement, God restored His relationship with sinful people by diverting their sin and judgment onto an innocent animal.

Looking Ahead

If you would like to prepare in advance for the next session, read Isaiah 55:1–7. It describes God's free offer to all who will accept it. Reflect on exactly what is being offered, and consider the price. Does it sound appealing to you?

Key Number Four

THE INVITATION

SETTING THE SCENE

*A*FTER His people wandered forty years in the desert, God led them into the promised land of Canaan. God remained with His people: He raised up leaders in times of crisis and gave the people victory over their enemies. But the people noticed that other countries had kings and standing armies, and they wanted to be the same. So God agreed to their request.

The first king, Saul, was a great disappointment, but under the leadership of his successor, David, God's blessing was evident. God promised that one of David's descendants would establish a kingdom that would last forever (1 Chronicles 17:11–12).

That promise is of great importance. Remember that the whole Bible story is about someone who would come to reverse the traumatic effects of what happened in the Garden of Eden.

God had promised that God's blessing would come through the line of Abraham. Now, we are told more specifically about God's blessing on a descendant of King David. This is why the rest of the Old Testament concentrates on David's family line.

After the death of David's son Solomon, the kingdom divided in two. Ten tribes in the north declared independence from the line of David. They suffered from poor leadership and were eventually overrun in the year 722 B.C.

Two tribes continued in the south. Some of their kings honored God; others led the people into evil. God spoke to the kings and the people through prophets who heard the word of God directly as Abraham and Moses had done before.

One of these prophets was Isaiah. It was through him that God issued a special invitation.

THE DIVIDED KINGDOM

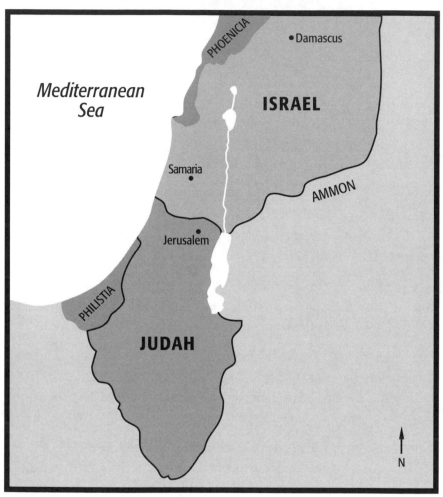

The ten northern tribes of Israel seceded from the nation. The two tribes in the south became known as Judah. The northern kingdom of Israel was captured and destroyed in 722 B.C. The southern kingdom, including Jerusalem, was destroyed in 586 B.C.

DATES	EVENTS	BOOKS OF THE BIBLE	WORLD HISTORY
	Creation	Genesis	
	The Flood		
			Construction of pyramids begins in Egypt (2650 B.C.)
		Job	
2000 B.C.	Abraham	Genesis	Metalworkers create bronze, ushering in Bronze Age
	Isaac		
	Jacob		
	Four Hundred Years of Slavery in Egypt	Exodus	
1500 B.C.	Exodus from Egypt (Moses)	Exodus, Leviticus, Numbers, Deuteronomy	Egyptians begin using parchment for writing
	Entrance into Canaan (Joshua)	Joshua	
	Three Hundred Years of Chaos (the Judges)	Judges Ruth	King Tut buried with fabulous treasures in Egypt
1000 B.C.	King Saul King David King Solomon	1 and 2 Samuel, 1 and 2 Kings, 1 Chronicles (Psalms, Proverbs, Ecclesiastes, Song of Songs)	
	Divided Kingdom (930 B.C.)	Isaiah, Jeremiah, Lamentations, Ezekiel, Daniel and the Minor Prophets	First Olympic Games held at Olympia in Greece
500 B.C.	Fall of Jerusalem and exile		Aesop becomes famous for his fables
	Rebuilding of Jerusalem (Ezra, Nehemiah)	Ezra, Nehemiah, Esther	Plato born in Greece
			Great Wall of China completed
4 B.C.	Birth of Christ		

FOLLOWING ALONG

INTRODUCTION:
There are many voices in the marketplace trying to attract your attention.

I. The Product.

A. The mysterious trader makes a remarkable offer.

Come, all you who are thirsty, come to the waters; and you who have no money, come, buy and eat!

Come, buy wine and milk without money and without cost. (Isaiah 55:1)

B. Jesus claims that He can satisfy the deepest thirsts of the soul.

If anyone is thirsty, let him come to me and drink. (John 7:37)

C. Since being evicted from the garden, human beings have had a desperate thirst.

In this world's marketplace, we scramble around to different stalls, desperately trying to find fulfillment, meaning, and satisfaction.

II. The Price Is Right.

A. The seller presides over a strange auction where the product goes to the lowest bidder.

Come, buy . . . without money and without cost. (Isaiah 55:1)

B. There is nothing we can offer God in payment for His priceless gift. He chooses to give it to us freely and only on that basis.

III. How Do You Make the Purchase?

    A. What Christ offers at no cost to us was obtained at great cost to Him.

    B. Buying indicates a definite transaction. There must be a definite transaction in which you take what He offers, and it actually becomes yours.

        1. Looking isn't buying.

        2. Trying isn't buying.

        3. Knowing isn't buying.

IV. Would You Like to Buy?

    A. Christ says, "Come, buy without money, without price." You could close that deal and receive what Christ offers today.

    B. Are you ready to buy? If so, make this prayer your own:

> Almighty God, thank You that Jesus Christ has come and purchased the gift of everlasting life with You.
>
> Thank You that He offers all this to me freely. Forgive me for my pride in thinking that there is something that I could offer in payment for such a gift.
>
> Humbly, I acknowledge I have nothing to offer You. My hand is empty, but it is therefore open to receive. Gladly, I receive what You freely give, believing Your promise and taking You at Your word, amazed that what You purchased at such cost may so freely and wonderfully become mine.
>
> Words cannot express the debt that I owe You. Fill my heart with Your love. Lead me now from this day in Your paths. Let me live for Your glory, through Jesus Christ my Savior and my Lord, in whose name I pray. Amen.

DISCUSSING TOGETHER

1. What is your immediate reaction when you hear of a free offer? Why?

2. What signs do you see in people around you that they are "thirsty"?

3. Would you say the deepest thirsts of your soul are being satisfied? If so, how are they being satisfied?

4. What do you think keeps people from accepting God's free offer to satisfy their souls?

5. In the auction analogy, we imagined people offering different "bids" for forgiveness and eternal life with God. What "bids" do you think most people are counting on to get into heaven?

_____

_____

_____

_____

_____

_____

_____

_____

6. _For personal reflection:_ Where are you in the purchase process right now—looking, trying, knowing, ready to buy, or already made the purchase? What would it take to make you ready to buy?

_____

_____

_____

_____

_____

_____

_____

_____

_____

_____

_____

_____

Building the Story

THE INVITATION:
God offers to meet the deepest needs of the human heart through Jesus Christ, but this offer must be received with empty hands.

Looking Ahead

If you would like to prepare in advance for next week, read Luke 1:26–80, which describes the events leading up to Jesus' birth. Notice Jesus' ties to Abraham and David. Look for hints as to what Jesus' mission will be.

Key Number Five

THE MANGER

SETTING THE SCENE

$\mathcal{S}$OME people responded to God's great invitation, but many turned to idols instead. God warned them that they would be overrun by their enemies.

In the year 586 B.C. the Babylonian army destroyed Jerusalem. Many died, a few fled, and the rest were taken as exiles into Babylon. While there, God's people began to seek Him in a new way.

After seventy years of living in exile, a small group returned to Jerusalem to rebuild the city and its temple. But the ark of the covenant, the centerpiece of worship in the Old Testament, was lost and despite the efforts of Indiana Jones, it has never been found!

Previously, God's visible presence had come to the temple on the Day of Atonement in the form of a cloud. But nothing like this happened in the new temple. The people must have longed that God would come to them as He had before.

The Old Testament story explains the human problem and announces God's promise to send someone who will deliver us from evil and restore us to the blessing and presence of God. But at the end of the Old Testament, the problem has not been solved and the promise has not yet been fulfilled. The curse announced in the garden stands and is the last word of the Old Testament.

So, for our fifth key, we turn to the New Testament. Here we are introduced to Jesus Christ.

Israel

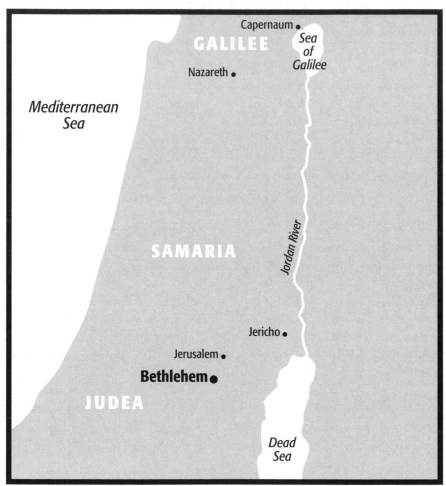

Caesar Augustus commisioned a census in Israel. Each family was required to register in the town of their ancestry. Joseph and Mary headed to Bethlehem, where Jesus was born in fulfillment of the prophecy in Micah 5:2.

DATES	EVENTS	BOOKS OF THE BIBLE	WORLD HISTORY
	Creation	Genesis	
	The Flood		Construction of pyramids begins in Egypt (2650 B.C.)
		Job	
2000 B.C.	Abraham	Genesis	Metalworkers create bronze, ushering in Bronze Age
	Isaac		
	Jacob		
	Four Hundred Years of Slavery in Egypt	Exodus	
1500 B.C.	Exodus from Egypt (Moses)	Exodus, Leviticus, Numbers, Deuteronomy	Egyptians begin using parchment for writing
	Entrance into Canaan (Joshua)	Joshua	
	Three Hundred Years of Chaos (the Judges)	Judges Ruth	King Tut buried with fabulous treasures in Egypt
1000 B.C.	King Saul King David King Solomon	1 and 2 Samuel, 1 and 2 Kings, 1 Chronicles (Psalms, Proverbs, Ecclesiastes, Song of Songs)	
	Divided Kingdom (930 B.C.)	Isaiah, Jeremiah, Lamentations, Ezekiel, Daniel and the Minor Prophets	First Olympic Games held at Olympia in Greece
500 B.C.	Fall of Jerusalem and exile		Aesop becomes famous for his fables
	Rebuilding of Jerusalem (Ezra, Nehemiah)	Ezra, Nehemiah, Esther	Plato born in Greece
			Great Wall of China completed
	Birth of Christ		

FOLLOWING ALONG

I. Life on the Island Is No Longer Idyllic.

    A. God created you to know Him and to enjoy Him for eternity in His presence.

    B. Sin ruptured our relationship with God.

    C. Adam and Eve were driven out of paradise.

    D. We live in a fallen world which has a curse hanging over it.

    E. God has promised that help will come.

II. Jesus Christ Is Fully God.

    A. Jesus was born as a result of the direct initiative of God.

        The uniqueness of this event was that Mary was a virgin. The life in Mary's womb came to be there by a creative miracle of God.

        "The Holy Spirit will come upon you, and the power of the Most High will overshadow you. So the holy one to be born will be called the Son of God." (Luke 1:35)

    B. The Son of God existed with the Father before He was "conceived" in Mary.

        In the beginning was the Word, and the Word was with God, and the Word was God. He was with God in the beginning. The Word became flesh and made his dwelling among us. (John 1:1–2, 14)

    C. Only God can reconcile men and women to God.

III. Jesus Christ Is Fully Man.

A. In the Old Testament story, God appeared as a man. In the New Testament, God *became* a man in Jesus.

B. Only a man can bear the punishment for man's sin.

Jesus embraces both divinity and humanity, bringing the two together in Himself.

IV. Jesus Christ Is Holy.

The angel answered, "The Holy Spirit will come upon you, and the power of the Most High will overshadow you. So the holy one to be born will be called the Son of God." (Luke 1:35)

A. Jesus never sinned in action or attitude.

B. Jesus knows the full power of temptation.

Don't think that Jesus Christ's temptations were less than yours. Only Christ knows the full power of temptation, because He is the only one who has withstood the full force of the enemy's power.

C. Jesus is the one who can deliver us from the knowledge of evil.

Jesus Christ is unlike any other person who has ever lived. That is why He is able to do for us what no other person, teaching, or religion can do. Jesus Christ is God. He is man. And He is holy. He is the fulfillment of God's promise, and He is the answer to our problem.

DISCUSSING TOGETHER

1. How would you have reacted if you had found the bottles with the warnings inside?

2. The message in the bottle said, "Help is coming." Why do we need help?

3. What new insights into Jesus did you gain from this message?

4. If Jesus were a man but not God, what difference would it make? Why was it important for Jesus to be born rather than simply to "appear" at some point in human history?

5. If Jesus were God but not a man, what difference would it make?

_____

_____

_____

_____

_____

_____

6. What does it mean to say that Jesus is holy? How is He different from us? Can a person be holy if he or she is tempted?

_____

_____

_____

_____

_____

_____

_____

7. *For personal reflection:* If Jesus Christ could change your life, would you want Him to?

_____

_____

_____

_____

_____

_____

_____

Building the Story

THE MANGER:
Jesus Christ is fully God, fully man, and He is holy. This uniquely qualifies Him to reconcile men and women to God.

Looking Ahead

If you would like to prepare in advance, read about Jesus' death in Luke 23. Notice the way the various people reacted to Jesus. Reflect on why the thief on the cross reached out to Jesus and was promised entrance into paradise.

Key Number Six

THE CROSS

SETTING THE SCENE

*J*ESUS began His public ministry when He was about thirty years old. His message was simple: "Repent, for the kingdom of heaven is near" (Matthew 4:17). God was opening up access to heaven and inviting people to submit to His rule.

Jesus called twelve men to become His disciples and traveled with them throughout the northern part of Israel known as Galilee. He taught in the synagogues, delivered people from the power of demons, healed the sick, and preached the good news of the kingdom (Matthew 4:23–24).

As news about Jesus spread, opposition increased. Many found His claims threatening, and some began a plot to have Him killed. This did not take Jesus by surprise. He told His disciples that He had to go to Jerusalem to suffer and die. He also told them that, on the third day, He would rise again, but they did not understand what He was talking about.

One of Jesus' own disciples betrayed Him. A show trial followed in which false witnesses spoke against Him. The Roman governor should have upheld the process of law, but instead he asked the people what should be done with Jesus. They called for Him to be crucified. The governor handed Him over to the people, and He was crucified on a cross between two criminals.

In this sixth session, we will discover how Jesus' death on the cross was the means by which God fulfilled all that He had promised in the Old Testament.

GOLGOTHA

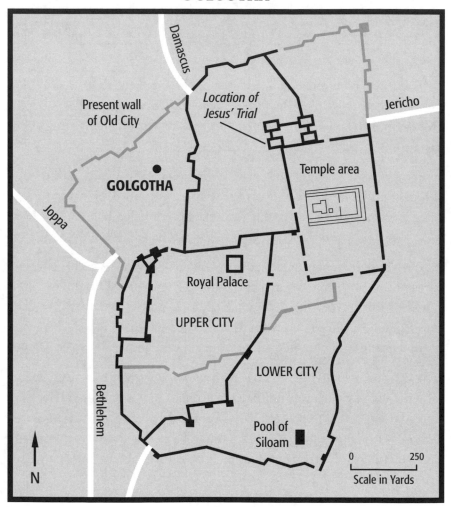

Jesus traveled to Jerusalem, the capital city and center of religious authority. It was here that Jesus was arrested and sentenced to death. He was crucified at Golgotha, just outside the city walls.

DATES	EVENTS	BOOKS OF THE BIBLE	WORLD HISTORY
4 B.C.	Birth of Christ	Matthew, Mark, Luke, John	
A.D. 10	Jesus raised in Nazareth		
A.D. 20			
A.D. 30	Jesus' ministry begins		Augustus becomes Emperor of Rome and brings peace
	Jesus crucified and risen The church is launched	Acts	
A.D. 40	The apostle Paul's first missionary journey		
A.D. 50	Paul and other disciples write letters to instruct and encourage the churches (These were written between	Romans, 1 and 2 Corinthians, Galatians, Ephesians, Philippians, Colossians, 1 and 2 Thessalonians, 1 and 2 Timothy, Titus,	
A.D. 60	A.D. 50 and 75)	Philemon, Hebrews, James, 1 and 2 Peter, 1, 2, and 3 John, Jude	
A.D. 70	Jerusalem destroyed		Christians brutally persecuted under Nero
A.D. 80			Construction of Colosseum at Rome
A.D. 90	The apostle John exiled to the island of Patmos and records Revelation, circa A.D. 95	Revelation	

Historians disagree as to the exact year of Christ's birth, offering dates ranging from 6 B.C. to A.D. 2.
All dates are approximate.

FOLLOWING ALONG

INTRODUCTION:

    A. God shows His love for you in the death of Jesus.

       God demonstrates his own love for us in this: While we were still sinners, Christ died for us. (Romans 5:8)

    B. Death is only an expression of love if something significant is accomplished. So what did Jesus achieve for us in His death?

I. Christ's Death Released Forgiveness.

    A. In the garden, the curse was diverted to the ground.

    B. God's justice says where there is sin, there must also be judgment.

    C. God's mercy allows the judgment for our sin to be diverted away from us.

    D. Jesus allowed God's judgment to fall on Him.

II. Christ's Death Opened Paradise.

    A. Adam and Eve were driven out of Paradise.

    B. One of the criminals realized it was time to get serious.

      1. He feared God

        "Don't you fear God?" (Luke 23:40)

      2. He recognized his sinful condition.

        "We are punished justly, for we are getting what our deeds deserve." (Luke 23:41)

      3. He believed on the Lord Jesus Christ.

        " . . . when you come into your kingdom." (Luke 23:42)

4. He asked Jesus to save him.

"Jesus, remember me when you come into your kingdom."
(Luke 23:42)

5. He rested on the words of Jesus.

"I tell you the truth, today you will be with me in paradise."
(Luke 23:43)

III. Christ's Death Subdued Death.

A. Jesus entered into all the dimensions of hell as the sins of the world were laid on Him.

B. Jesus endured the wrath of God.

"My God, my God, why have you forsaken me?" (Mark 15:34)

C. Jesus died in triumph.

When he had received the drink, Jesus said, "It is finished." With that, he bowed his head and gave up his spirit. (John 19:30)

Jesus called out with a loud voice, "Father, into your hands I commit my spirit." (Luke 23:46)

D. Jesus has made the valley of death a safe place for His people.

IV. Answer These Five Life-Changing Questions.

A. Do you fear God?

B. Do you recognize your sinful condition?

C. Do you believe in the Lord Jesus Christ?

D. Have you asked Him to save you?

E. Do you trust His Word, His promise?

DISCUSSING TOGETHER

1. What is one of the most loving things someone has done for you? In what ways was it loving? How did you feel when you received this demonstration of love?

_____

_____

_____

_____

2. What insights did you gain about Jesus' death from the video presentation?

_____

_____

_____

3. Give an example of a time when you either saw or experienced justice. Give an example when you were given mercy instead of justice. How did you feel when you were shown mercy?

_____

_____

_____

_____

_____

_____

4. How does Christ's dying on a cross fulfill God's justice and mercy at the same time?

_____

_____

_____

_____

_____

5. What would people have to understand about themselves in order for the message of the Cross to seem relevant to them?

_____

_____

_____

_____

6. _For personal reflection:_ Did anything hinder you from answering yes to any of the questions at the end of the talk (point IV in the outline)? If so, what? If you answered yes, for the first time, to each of the five questions, consider sharing your decision with someone.

_____

_____

_____

_____

_____

_____

_____

Building the Story

THE CROSS:
Christ's death released forgiveness, as the judgment due us was diverted onto Him.

Looking Ahead

We end this session with Christ on the cross, but that is not the end of the story. If you would like to prepare in advance for session seven, read Luke 24:1–12. Consider whether you would have believed Mary when she came back to the disciples with the big news.

Key Number Seven

THE TOMB

SETTING THE SCENE

*W*HEN Jesus died, a man called Joseph went to Pilate and asked for the body of Jesus (Matthew 27:58).

Pilate wanted to be certain that Jesus was dead, so he summoned the centurion, who had supervised the crucifixion. After receiving the centurion's confirmation that Jesus was dead, Pilate released the body of Jesus to Joseph (Mark 15:44–45).

Joseph wrapped the body of Jesus in strips of linen. He owned a tomb in the garden near the place where Jesus had been crucified. Christ's body was laid in the tomb, and a stone was rolled in front of the entrance.

The women who had been at the foot of the cross followed Joseph in order to see where Christ had been buried. Then they hurried home in order to prepare spices and perfumes that they would use to anoint the dead body of Christ (Luke 23:55–56).

The Pharisees remembered Jesus' declaration that He would rise again, so they lobbied Pilate to provide a guard at the tomb. Pilate instructed them to "make the tomb as secure as you know how" (Matthew 27:65).

But on the third day, the tomb was empty. Jesus had risen.

JERUSALEM AND GALILEE

Jesus rose from the dead on the third day and appeared to His disciples in Jerusalem and Galilee.

DATES	EVENTS	BOOKS OF THE BIBLE	WORLD HISTORY
4 B.C.	Birth of Christ	Matthew, Mark, Luke, John	
A.D. 10	Jesus raised in Nazareth		
A.D. 20			
A.D. 30	Jesus' ministry begins		Augustus becomes Emperor of Rome and brings peace
	Jesus crucified and risen The church is launched	Acts	
A.D. 40	The apostle Paul's first missionary journey		
A.D. 50	Paul and other disciples write letters to instruct and encourage the churches (These were written between	Romans, 1 and 2 Corinthians, Galatians, Ephesians, Philippians, Colossians, 1 and 2 Thessalonians, 1 and 2 Timothy, Titus,	
A.D. 60	A.D. 50 and 75)	Philemon, Hebrews, James, 1 and 2 Peter, 1, 2, and 3 John, Jude	Christians brutally persecuted under Nero
A.D. 70	Jerusalem destroyed		
A.D. 80			Construction of Colosseum at Rome
A.D. 90	The apostle John exiled to the island of Patmos and records Revelation, circa A.D. 95	Revelation	

Historians disagree as to the exact year of Christ's birth, offering dates ranging from 6 B.C. to A.D. 2.
All dates are approximate.

FOLLOWING ALONG

Introduction:
A. The women did not know what to make of the empty tomb.

Their faith had been crushed as they witnessed the awful suffering and death of Jesus. Sometimes terrible experiences of suffering make it hard to believe.

B. God gave the explanation of the empty tomb.

"Why do you look for the living among the dead? He is not here; he has risen!" (Luke 24:5b–6)

C. A Christian is a person who believes God's explanation of His own actions.

Christian faith does not rest on your feelings or on your interpretation of events. It is about believing God's explanation of events.

I. "Risen" Means that Death Is Defeated.
A. By His death, Jesus changed the nature of death.

From the time of Adam until the time of Christ, death had a way in but no way out. But Christ cut a hole in death!

B. For those who believe, death is not a prison but a passageway into the presence of God.

II. "Risen" Means Your Whole Person Will Be Redeemed.
A. The message of Easter is not that Jesus is alive, but that Jesus is *risen!*

Jesus could have returned to the Father in His Spirit, and continued the life He shared with the Father before He was born into the world. But He didn't do that because He came to save every part of you—soul and body—from the power of sin and death.

B. You are a union of body and soul together, and so death, which separates the body and the soul, is the undoing of your nature.

C. The only way in which death can be defeated is for your body and soul to be reunited in the power of a new life.

D. God does not offer to bring a part of you into heaven. He wants you to be there—every part of you—soul and body.

III. **"Risen" means that we will all be changed.**

A. When the body of Jesus was raised, it was also changed.

1. The disciples knew and recognized Jesus, but His body was adapted in a way that was appropriate for eternal life.

2. When Lazarus was raised from the dead, he continued life as before and eventually faced death again! But the resurrected body of Jesus is no longer subject to aging, pain, or death.

3. This is the glorious future for every Christian believer.

B. When a Christian believer dies, the body is buried, but the soul goes immediately and consciously into the presence of Christ.

C. All believers will receive the gift of the resurrection body at the same time when Jesus comes again.

DISCUSSING TOGETHER

1. How have you viewed and celebrated Easter in the past? In what ways has this presentation changed your perspective of Easter?

2. How would you have responded if you had arrived at the tomb and found it empty? What would it have taken to convince you that Jesus had truly risen?

3. What difference would it have made if Jesus had not risen from the dead? What if He had risen in spirit but not in body?

4. Describe your view of life after death. In what ways has your view changed after this presentation?

_____

_____

_____

_____

_____

_____

5. How does Christ's resurrection make Christianity different from other religions?

_____

_____

_____

_____

_____

6. _For personal reflection:_ How does Jesus' resurrection from the dead bolster your faith or lead you closer to trusting Him as your Savior?

_____

_____

_____

_____

_____

_____

Building the Story

THE TOMB:
Jesus' resurrection demonstrates that He has overcome the power of death and that He is able to give eternal life to your soul and body.

Looking Ahead

If you would like to prepare in advance for next week, read Acts 2. Imagine that you were a reporter covering these events. What would your headline have been for the next day's paper?

Key Number Eight

THE SPIRIT

SETTING THE SCENE

*T*HE Bible records at least nine occasions when Jesus appeared to one or more of His disciples after His resurrection. These appearances demonstrated to the disciples that Jesus was indeed alive.

One of these appearances was to a group of more than five hundred witnesses (1 Corinthians 15:6). The story was verifiable because many of these witnesses were still alive when Paul wrote about the event.

After a period of forty days, Jesus went to the Mount of Olives with His disciples. He commissioned them to go and make disciples of all the nations and promised them His continuing presence. But their immediate instructions were to wait in Jerusalem. Jesus had taught them about the Holy Spirit. Now He promised that the Spirit would come.

Then Jesus ascended into heaven. The disciples saw Him go. He was taken into the cloud, which in the Old Testament represented the presence of God. He was returning to His Father.

The disciples went back to Jerusalem and waited. On the Day of Pentecost, the Holy Spirit came to the disciples in a dramatic fashion.

In the Old Testament, the Holy Spirit was given to a few people for particular tasks. But since the death and resurrection of Jesus, the Holy Spirit is given to everybody who believes in Him.

NATIONS OF THE PENTECOSTAL FESTIVAL

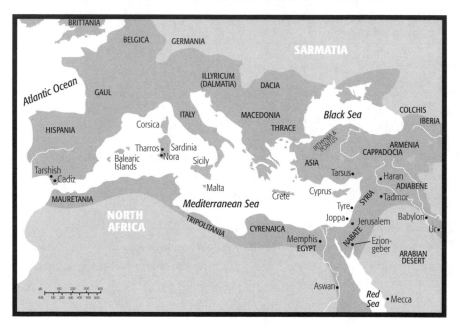

Thousands of Jews had come to Jerusalem for the annual Festival of the Pentecost. After the Spirit descended on the disciples they spoke to the multicultural crowd in their own languages.

Dates	Events	Books of the Bible	World History
4 B.C.	Birth of Christ	Matthew, Mark, Luke, John	
A.D. 10	Jesus raised in Nazareth		
A.D. 20			
A.D. 30	Jesus' ministry begins		Augustus becomes Emperor of Rome and brings peace
	Jesus crucified and risen The church is launched	Acts	
A.D. 40	The apostle Paul's first missionary journey		
A.D. 50	Paul and other disciples write letters to instruct and encourage the churches (These were written between	Romans, 1 and 2 Corinthians, Galatians, Ephesians, Philippians, Colossians, 1 and 2 Thessalonians, 1 and 2 Timothy, Titus,	
A.D. 60	A.D. 50 and 75)	Philemon, Hebrews, James, 1 and 2 Peter, 1, 2, and 3 John, Jude	Christians brutally persecuted under Nero
A.D. 70	Jerusalem destroyed		
A.D. 80			Construction of Colosseum at Rome
A.D. 90	The apostle John exiled to the island of Patmos and records Revelation, circa A.D. 95	Revelation	

Historians disagree as to the exact year of Christ's birth, offering dates ranging from 6 B.C. to A.D. 2.
All dates are approximate.

FOLLOWING ALONG

INTRODUCTION:

The nature of God is a mystery beyond our grasp.

What the Bible reveals about God is best summarized in three statements: 1. There is one God. 2. God exists in three persons—the Father, the Son, and the Holy Spirit. 3. Each person is fully God.

Christians do not believe in three Gods. The one eternal God is Father, Son, and Holy Spirit.

I. The Holy Spirit Leads People to Faith in Christ.

A. The Holy Spirit disturbs.

When he [The Holy Spirit] comes, he will convict the world of guilt in regard to sin. (John 16:8)

B. The Holy Spirit illuminates.

The Spirit is like a floodlight shining on Jesus Christ, to illuminate the truth about Him (see John 15:26).

C. The Holy Spirit indwells.

The Holy Spirit is given to everyone who comes to believe in Jesus. He is with you and in you (see John 14:17).

II. The Holy Spirit Descended upon True Believers on the Day of Pentecost.

A. Believers heard a sound like the wind.

When the day of Pentecost came, they were all together in one place. Suddenly a sound like the blowing of a violent wind came from heaven and filled the whole house where they were sitting. (Acts 2:1–2)

God breathes out new life by the power of His Holy Spirit, making people alive to God.

B. Believers saw what looked like fire.

They saw what seemed to be tongues of fire that separated and came to rest on each of them. (v. 3)

God gives the Holy Spirit to every believer, because He wants each one to play a role in advancing His purpose in the world.

C. Believers spoke in other languages.

All of them were filled with the Holy Spirit and began to speak in other tongues as the Spirit enabled them. (v. 4)

This miracle demonstrated that God wants all people to hear the good news about Jesus.

III. The Holy Spirit Empowers All Believers Today.

A. The wind teaches me that God's Spirit can make me alive to Him.

B. The fire tells me that God will equip and use me to serve Him.

C. The languages tell me that God wants me to play a part in bringing the good news of Jesus to all people.

DISCUSSING TOGETHER

1. What would have particularly stood out to you if you had been observing the events surrounding the Spirit's arrival on the Day of Pentecost?

2. What new insights did you gain about the Holy Spirit from this message? How has it changed your perspective?

3. The Holy Spirit disturbs, illuminates, and indwells. What evidence, if any, have you seen of the Holy Spirit in your life or in the life of someone else?

4. What would you like to see the Holy Spirit do in your life?

5. How do you feel about having God live in you through the Holy Spirit?

6. God gifts and empowers every believer so that each one can play a part in His purpose. Can you see any ways in which God is doing this through you or through the lives of other Christians?

Building the Story

THE SPIRIT:
The Holy Spirit makes us alive to God and empowers us to serve God in the world.

Looking Ahead

Read Romans 7:14–8:14, a passage that contrasts a life of defeat with a life of victory over temptation. Note the characteristics of both.

Key Number Nine

THE FIGHT

SETTING THE SCENE

*A*FTER the Day of Pentecost, the church continued to grow. The lives of the early believers were marked by unusual joy, and their love for one another drew attention to the authenticity of their message.

But it was not long before these believers faced persecution for their faith in Christ. They were scattered, and in this way the Good News began to spread. God had promised that all the nations of the earth would be blessed through Abraham, and it was through these first Jewish believers that the good news about Jesus began to spread around the earth.

Saul of Tarsus led a furious campaign of persecution against Christians until God miraculously intervened in his life, bringing him to faith in Christ. The church's most bitter opponent became her greatest pioneer, and we know him better as the apostle Paul.

The Holy Spirit revealed truth to Paul directly, just as He had to the prophets in the Old Testament. In this way the great truths of the Christian faith were committed to writing in Paul's letters that form an important part of the New Testament.

One of these is the book of Romans. Here, Paul explains that in Jesus Christ, God not only forgives our sins but also gives us the power to live a new life that is pleasing to Him. Jesus came not only to save us from sin's penalty but also from its power, and He never does the one without the other.

In this lesson, we will discover that the Christian life is a fight. We are at war with the sin that lurks within us. But this is a winnable war, and that's our ninth key for Unlocking the Bible.

PAUL'S MISSIONARY JOURNEYS

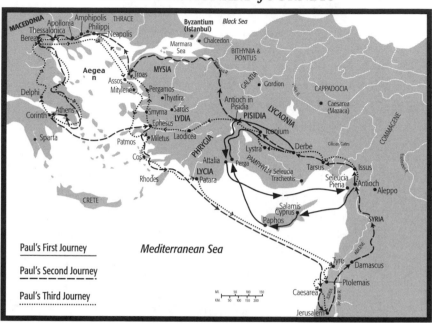

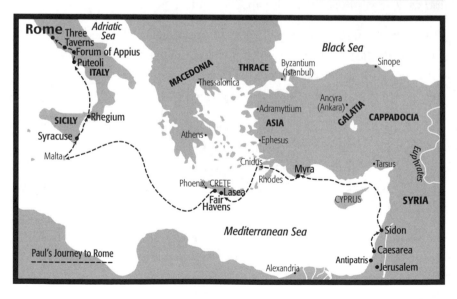

The apostle Paul made a series of missionary journeys in ever-widening circles to take the good news of Jesus Christ to the world.

DATES	EVENTS	BOOKS OF THE BIBLE	WORLD HISTORY
4 B.C.	Birth of Christ	Matthew, Mark, Luke, John	
A.D. 10	Jesus raised in Nazareth		
A.D. 20			
A.D. 30	Jesus' ministry begins		Augustus becomes Emperor of Rome and brings peace
	Jesus crucified and risen The church is launched	Acts	
A.D. 40	The apostle Paul's first missionary journey		
A.D. 50	Paul and other disciples write letters to instruct and encourage the churches (These were written between	Romans, 1 and 2 Corinthians, Galatians, Ephesians, Philippians, Colossians, 1 and 2 Thessalonians, 1 and 2 Timothy, Titus,	
A.D. 60	A.D. 50 and 75)	Philemon, Hebrews, James, 1 and 2 Peter, 1, 2, and 3 John, Jude	Christians brutally persecuted under Nero
A.D. 70	Jerusalem destroyed		
A.D. 80			Construction of Colosseum at Rome
A.D. 90	The apostle John exiled to the island of Patmos and records Revelation, circa A.D. 95	Revelation	

Historians disagree as to the exact year of Christ's birth, offering dates ranging from 6 B.C. to A.D. 2.
All dates are approximate.

FOLLOWING ALONG

INTRODUCTION:

When God saves us in Jesus Christ, He deals with both the penalty and the power of sin.

I. **Meet Three Characters —**
   Hostile, Helpless, and Hopeful — based upon Romans 7–8.

   A. Hostile has neither the desire nor the ability to obey God.

   > *The sinful mind is hostile to God. It does not submit to God's law, nor can it do so. (Romans 8:7)*

   B. Helpless has the desire to obey God, but he does not have the ability.

   > *In my inner being I delight in God's law. (Romans 7:22)*

   > *I see another law at work in the members of my body, waging war against the law of my mind and making me a prisoner of the law of sin. . . . What a wretched man I am! Who will rescue me from this body of death? (Romans 7:23–24)*

   C. Hopeful has the desire and the ability to obey God.

   > *Those who live in accordance with the Spirit have their minds set on what the Spirit desires. (Romans 8:5b)*

   > *By the Spirit you put to death the misdeeds of the body. (Romans 8:13b)*

   The Christian life is all about the proper application of overwhelming force, specifically the power of the Holy Spirit who is with you—and in you—when you are a Christian.

II. God Speaks to Hostile, Helpless, and Hopeful.

A. To Hostile: God loves you, so repent!

God demonstrates his own love for us in this: While we were still sinners, Christ died for us. (Romans 5:8)

B. To Helpless: Christ will rescue you, so come!

What a wretched man I am! Who will rescue me from this body of death? Thanks be to God—through Jesus Christ our Lord! (Romans 7:24–25)

C. To Hopeful: The Holy Spirit is in you, so fight!

If by the Spirit you put to death the misdeeds of the body, you will live. (Romans 8:13b)

III. Prayers of Response.

A. A Prayer for Hostile

"Lord, You know that I've been putting up a fight against You for a long time. But today instead of Your enemy, I want to become Your friend through the grace that is extended to me in Jesus Christ. Bring me over to Your side right now, I pray in Jesus' name. Amen."

B. A Prayer for Helpless

"Lord, You know that I've been struggling for a long time and trying to live a different life. I've not been succeeding and I realize now why. Today I put my trust in Jesus Christ. Lord, be my Savior, and be my deliverer by the power of Your Spirit from this moment. I pray this in Jesus' name. Amen."

C. A Prayer for Hopeful

"Lord, thank You that Your Spirit lives in me. Forgive me that sometimes I've talked or even thought as if I were still helpless. Thank You that I'm not because Your Spirit has put me in a position to fight. Lead me forward so that I may grow in the Christian life. Thank You for making me hopeful through Jesus Christ, my Lord. Amen."

DISCUSSING TOGETHER

1. Why do you think it is often so difficult to do what you know is right?

2. Describe the spiritual lives of the following categories of people.

	HOSTILE	HELPLESS	HOPEFUL
Desire to live a holy life	No	Yes	Yes
Ability to live a holy life	No	No	Yes
Bible passage	Romans 8:7	Romans 7:22–24	Romans 8:5, 13

3. Put an "X" on the paper or in your mind to indicate which character you relate to most closely. Which one would you like to be? (You don't need to answer this question out loud.)

4. What would you tell someone who saw himself as Helpless but wanted to be Hopeful? How about someone who was Hostile but wanted to be Hopeful?

_____

_____

_____

_____

_____

_____

_____

5. What advice would you give to Hopeful? How can we, in practical terms, apply the "overwhelming force" of the Holy Spirit to the sins we struggle with?

_____

_____

_____

_____

_____

_____

_____

_____

_____

_____

Building the Story

THE FIGHT:
The Christian life is a winnable war. The Holy Spirit enables you to make progress in the battle to live a life that is pleasing to God.

Looking Ahead

If you would like to prepare in advance for next time, read Revelation 21–22. Note the images of heaven that are particularly attractive to you.

Key Number Ten

THE CITY

SETTING THE STAGE

*I*N his old age, the apostle John was imprisoned on the island of Patmos on account of his faith in Jesus Christ. While he was there, God gave him a vision of the future, which is recorded in the book of Revelation.

John knew that Jesus had promised to come again. When Christ ascended, John had heard the angel confirm that Jesus would come in the same way as the apostles had seen Him go.

The Bible describes the dramatic conclusion of human history that will take place when Jesus Christ comes again. He will come—personally and visibly—and when He comes, He will bring all His people into His immediate presence.

The book of Revelation describes the magnificent future that lies ahead of every Christian believer. It is full of wonderful symbols that help us to grasp things that would otherwise be beyond our understanding.

The Bible makes clear that every person who has ever lived will see Jesus Christ and personally experience either heaven or hell. Jesus Christ will pronounce the final verdict on the life of every person.

Then God will create a new heaven and a new earth. This planet, so long under the curse pronounced in the garden, will finally be renewed and restored. Every trace of the knowledge of evil will be removed, and Jesus Christ will lead all His people into the joys of a new life that will eclipse even the Garden of Eden.

ISLAND OF PATMOS

The apostle John was exiled to the island of Patmos where God gave him a vision recorded in the book of Revelation.

Dates	Events	Books of the Bible	World History
4 B.C.	Birth of Christ	Matthew, Mark, Luke, John	
A.D. 10	Jesus raised in Nazareth		
A.D. 20			
A.D. 30	Jesus' ministry begins		Augustus becomes Emperor of Rome and brings peace
	Jesus crucified and risen The church is launched	Acts	
A.D. 40	The apostle Paul's first missionary journey		
A.D. 50	Paul and other disciples write letters to instruct and encourage the churches (These were written between	Romans, 1 and 2 Corinthians, Galatians, Ephesians, Philippians, Colossians, 1 and 2 Thessalonians, 1 and 2 Timothy, Titus,	
A.D. 60	A.D. 50 and 75)	Philemon, Hebrews, James, 1 and 2 Peter, 1, 2, and 3 John, Jude	Christians brutally persecuted under Nero
A.D. 70	Jerusalem destroyed		
A.D. 80			Construction of Colosseum at Rome
A.D. 90	The apostle John exiled to the island of Patmos and records Revelation, circa A.D. 95	Revelation	

Historians disagree as to the exact year of Christ's birth, offering dates ranging from 6 B.C. to A.D. 2.
All dates are approximate.

FOLLOWING ALONG

INTRODUCTION:

Then I saw a new heaven and a new earth. (Revelation 21:1)

Before the beginning of human history there was a rebellion in heaven. The new heaven and earth will be free from the presence and even the possibility of evil. Evil can never raise its ugly head again.

The creation itself will be liberated from its bondage to decay and brought into the glorious freedom of the children of God. (Romans 8:21)

I. The City

I saw the Holy City, the new Jerusalem, coming down out of heaven from God. (Revelation 21:2)

A. Jerusalem was God's designated place for worship in the Old Testament.

B. The Most Holy Place in the temple was constructed as a cube. This was where God met with the high priest on the Day of Atonement.

C. The dimensions of the New Jerusalem are also like a cube, signifying that this is the holy place, where God lives with all His people.

I did not see a temple in the city, because the Lord God Almighty and the Lamb are its temple. (Revelation 21:22)

"Now the dwelling of God is with men, and he will live with them. They will be his people, and God himself will be with them and be their God." (Revelation 21:3)

II. The Garden

Inside the city John sees a garden. This is paradise restored. All the gifts that Adam and Eve enjoyed in the Garden of Eden will be restored and surpassed in God's great garden city.

A. The Place

There is no tree of the knowledge of good and evil in God's garden city because evil can no longer be known.

There is access to the tree of life (see Revelation 22:2).

B. Our Purpose

Men and women are restored to their highest purpose.

His servants will serve him. (Revelation 22:3)

They will reign for ever and ever. (Revelation 22:5)

Reigning means that life will be ordered and brought under your control. Serving means that you will be able to fulfill all God's purposes freely and joyfully.

C. The People

The story began with one couple enjoying the Garden of Eden. It will end with a vast crowd from every nation sharing the joys of life together in God's great garden city.

D. God's Presence

The throne of God and of the Lamb will be in the city, and his servants will serve him. They will see his face. (Revelation 22:3–4)

III. Come and Be Blessed!

A. The Bible story ends with God's invitation to come and share what Christ has prepared for you.

The Spirit and the bride say, "Come!" (Revelation 22:17)

B. Those who belong to Christ are blessed.

"Blessed are those who wash their robes, that they may have the right to the tree of life and may go through the gates into the city." (Revelation 22:14)

DISCUSSING TOGETHER

1. How did you picture heaven before this message? How has your view changed?

_____

_____

_____

_____

_____

_____

2. What aspects of life in God's garden city appeal to you most?

_____

_____

_____

_____

_____

3. Do you expect to be in heaven? Why?

_____

_____

_____

_____

_____

_____

4. How has God been working in your life over the past ten weeks?

5. What would you most like to take away from this study?

Please take a few minutes to fill out the feedback form on page 109 and leave it with your group leader.

Building the Story

THE CITY:

Jesus Christ will lead all who follow Him into the joys of a perfect life in the presence of God.

BUILDING THE STORY POINTS

The Garden:
God created Adam and Eve in His image, but they chose to disobey him, gained the knowledge of evil, and were evicted from Paradise.

The Law:
The Ten Commandments reflect the character of God, identify our greatest struggles, and demonstrate our need for Jesus Christ.

The Sacrifice:
Through the Day of Atonement, God restored His relationship with sinful people by diverting their sin and judgment onto an innocent animal.

The Invitation:
God offers to meet the deepest needs of the human heart through Jesus Christ, but this offer must be received with empty hands.

The Manger:
Jesus Christ is fully God, fully man, and He is holy. This uniquely qualifies Him to reconcile men and women to God.

The Cross:
Christ's death released forgiveness, as the judgment due us was diverted onto Him.

The Tomb:
Jesus' resurrection demonstrates that He has overcome the power of death and that He is able to give eternal life to your soul and body.

The Spirit:
The Holy Spirit makes us alive to God and empowers us to serve God in the world.

The Fight:
The Christian life is a winnable war. The Holy Spirit enables you to make progress in the battle to live a life that is pleasing to God.

The City:
Jesus Christ will lead all who follow Him into the joys of a perfect life in the presence of God.

FEEDBACK FORM

Name:_____

1. Why did you decide to attend this *Ten Keys* course?

_____

2. What did you find most meaningful about your experience?

_____

3. How would you have described your spiritual condition before this study?

_____

4. How has this study impacted your spiritual life?

_____

5. What suggestions would you make for improving the study for next time?

_____

_____

6. Are you interested in participating in another Bible study?

_____

7. Additional comments:

_____

_____

_____

_____